# ANIMALS IN THE NEWS

# ANIMALS IN THE NEWS

### CREATED BY RICHARD CRYSTAL

#### CAPTIONS WRITTEN BY
#### BILL MARICH AND RICH ROSS

**WARNER BOOKS**

An AOL Time Warner Company

COPYRIGHT © 2003 BY TK
ALL RIGHTS RESERVED

WARNER BOOKS, INC. 1271 AVENUE OF THE AMERICAS, NEW YORK, NY 10020
VISIT OUR WEB SITE AT WWW.TWBOOKMARK.COM.

 An AOL Time Warner Company

PRINTED IN THE UNITED STATES OF AMERICA

FIRST PRINTING: AUGUST 2003
10 9 8 7 6 5 4 3 2 1

LIBRARY OF CONGRESS CATALOGING-IN-PUBLICATION DATA

COVER AND INTERIOR BOOK DESIGN BY CLAIRE BROWN

THIS BOOK IS DEDICATED TO

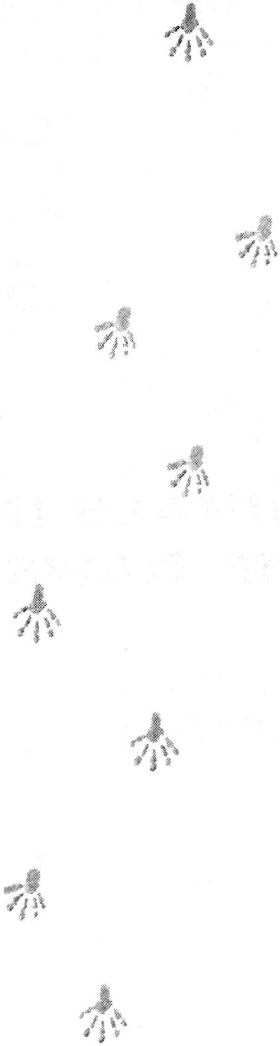

# ANIMALS IN THE NEWS

than
much

 its are
has re-
Ground-
en the
rodent

re
ng
eh
t
n
no

ser
nia
ct,
rd,
p,
t

leased yesterday snow.

**After staying** unmarried for nearly seventy-five years, perennial bachelor Dick Spellers finally stopped holding out for supermodels and agreed to meet on a blind date.

**Work began yesturday** for school-age volunteers who had gathered to begin inflating the giant elephant floats for this year's Macy's Thanksgiving Day Parade.

**Years before** applying her communication techniques on Helen Keller, famed socialworker Anne Sullivan honed her skills on Buster, the world's only signing dog.

**Thanks to a major ACLU court victory,** it is now illegal for the Rockettes to turn away any dancer just because she refuses to shave her legs.

**In Westport, Virginia,** Chuckie the Chicken filed a multimillion-dollar discrimination lawsuit after he was stopped by a bouncer and refused entry into a popular cat bar.

**The Yarnish family** of Helmanntown, Tennesse, filed suit against a local kennel yesterday when they learned that the pointer they had adopted to keep their two-year-old Boxer company was actually a four year old girl.

**Jimmy Briskel** of North Hamton, Massachusetts, learned a valuable lesson about making friends on the Internet yesterday when the girl who described herself only as "cool young 'hottie' 19" showed up at his door.

**After a poll** of thousands of visitors, the winner of the "ugliest animal in the zoo" was announced yesterday.  However, one pollster commented."He probably wouldn't be so bad without the hat."

leased yesterday show.

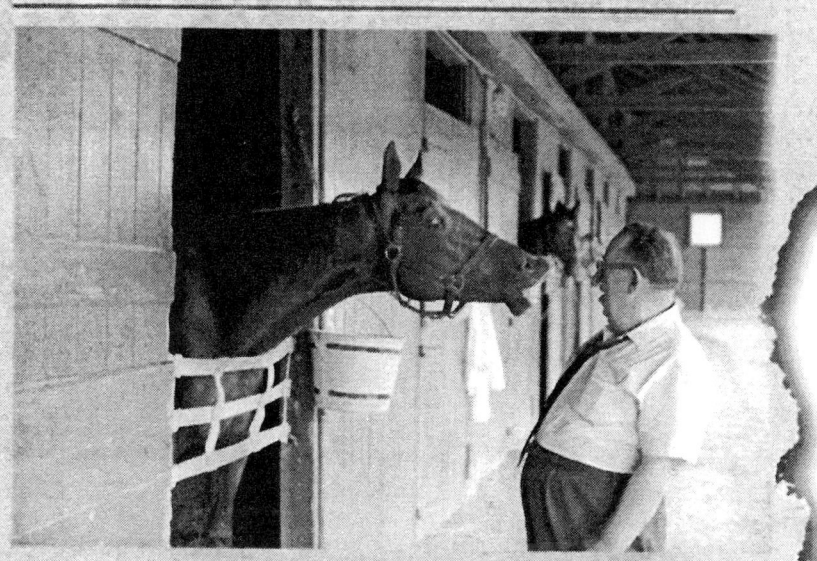

**Thoroughbred racehorse** "Honest to Goodness" showed his displeasure after learning that this three hundred pound guy was going to ride him in the next race.

**David Fesch,** founding member of the proverbial "Barrel of Monkeys," retired today after seventy-five years. When asked why, Fesch stated that "relaxing was simply *more fun* than a barrel of monkeys."

**The purity of Los Angels'** water supply came into question yesterday when strange foreign objects suddenly began pouring from people's taps.

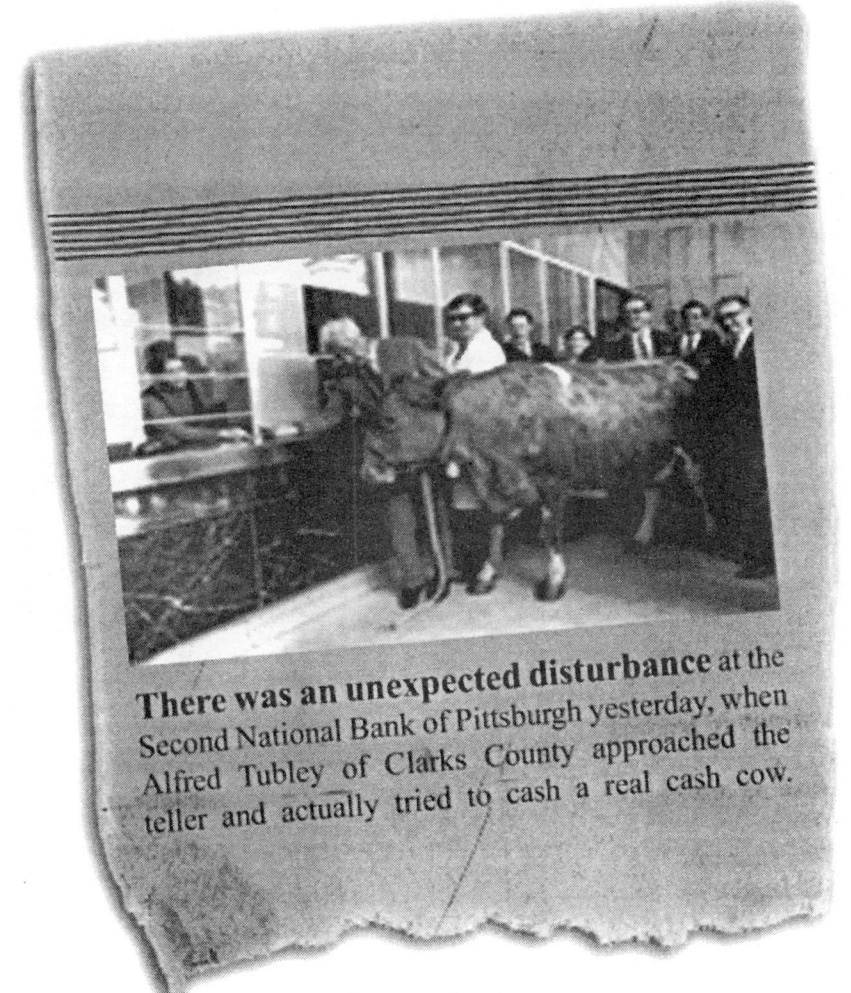

**There was an unexpected disturbance** at the Second National Bank of Pittsburgh yesterday, when Alfred Tubley of Clarks County approached the teller and actually tried to cash a real cash cow.

**Sick and tired** of singing that silly song over and over again, successful novelty toy Billy the Singing Bass wriggled off his plague yesterday and went on a psychotic rampage.

**Cast members** of the latest *Babe* sequel were personally escorted out of a posh New York City hotel yesterday, for berating bellhops and vandalizing ice machines.

**The art world** was shaken this week when this photo turned up, identifying the real artist behind 95 percent of all modern art.

MISSING PHOTO

**This weekend,** little Jimmy Dempski of Tresdale, Ohio, suffered minor emotional trauma when a local baby photographer told him to watch the birdie— then suddenly mauled and ate it.

**Just when it was thought** to have finally clean up its act, controversy again surrounds an Orange County infertility clinic.

**Last week,** news magazine *60 Minutes* took their hidden cameras into a well-known car dealership and revealed that while humans change the oil, small ponies are actually responsible for most of the mechanical labor.

MISSING PHOTO

**A famous cable infomercial spokeswoman** sued a major pharmaceutical company this week for complications *she* claims she experienced with that company's antiwrinkle cream.

leased yesterday snow.

than
much

ats are
has re-
ground-
n the
odent

re
ng
eh
ot
in
no

ser
nia
et.
rd,
p.

**In St. Louis yesterday,** Todd the Mackerel broke the species barrier by becoming baseball's first National League umpire.

**In Ashton, Wyoming,** an odd accident happened last night when five circus monkeys were in the middle of filming a TV commercial for Super Glue.

**At Texas State Fair** this week, little Johhny McWerther, of Abilene introduced a new game to replace the recently banned cow chip-tossing contest.

**In an attempt to bolster their image,** the dogs from the famous poker painting reunited last week in Marion, Michigan, to pose for this recreation of Da Vinci's *Last Supper*.

**During their annual conference,** dermatologists in Eunice, New Mexico, released this dramatic photo emphasizing the importance of a good sunscreen.

**Investigative reporters** overseas snapped this disturbing photo at a French bottled water company. Here we see a local worker drawing water from the so-called "mountain spring."

**The National Convention of Lazy People** met Wednesday in Taneytown, Maryland, for their annual horseback riding gala.

**The State Highway and Saftly Commission** ruled today that a dog can be fined $700 for allowing his human to stick his hand out of the window while he's driving.

**Whispers the cat** was unanimously voted out of obedience school this week for constantly reminding the teacher, five minutes before the bell, that she forgot to give everybody homework.

**The chimp on the left** is both amazed and shocked. It seems as though he just made it into the *Guinness Book of World Records* for passing the largest gall stone.

MISSING PHOTO

**Veterinarians** at the Milburn Zoo yesterday discovered the reason Roddy the alligator had been coughing for six months. Evidently, he had an actual frog in this throat.

**Emergency drills** were held over the weekend for K-9 citizens of Osaka, Japan, who are trained at an early age to hide beneath more structurally sound dogs in the event of an earthquake.

**And yesterday** in Trebertsville, Ohio, audiences were treated to the premier showing of Lassie's first 3-D movie.

**In Uma, Vermont,** the St. Martin's Church dance marathon ended after twenty-four hours, leaving only these two contestants, who were later disqualified for doing the Lambada... the forbidden dance of love.

**After the release** of this graphic photo, the International Conference of Genetic Scientists called an emergency meeting to ban the cloning of laboratory mice and Penn hard-court tennis balls.

**The annual** stuff-a-cat-in-a-trophy contest took place in Deer Park, New Jersey, this weekend. This was *not* one of the winners, because you can still see the head.

MISSING PHOTO

**A reward** of five hundred dollars is being offered to anyone who can find boxing promoter Don King's missing dog.

**A new study revealed** that women who routinely ride horses together have biological clocks that sync up so precisely that they actually experience morning sickness at the same exact moment each day. That study did nothing to explain the guy on the far right.

**Production continued** this week on a host of Hollywood Westerns, inspite of a walkout by hundreds of union horses.

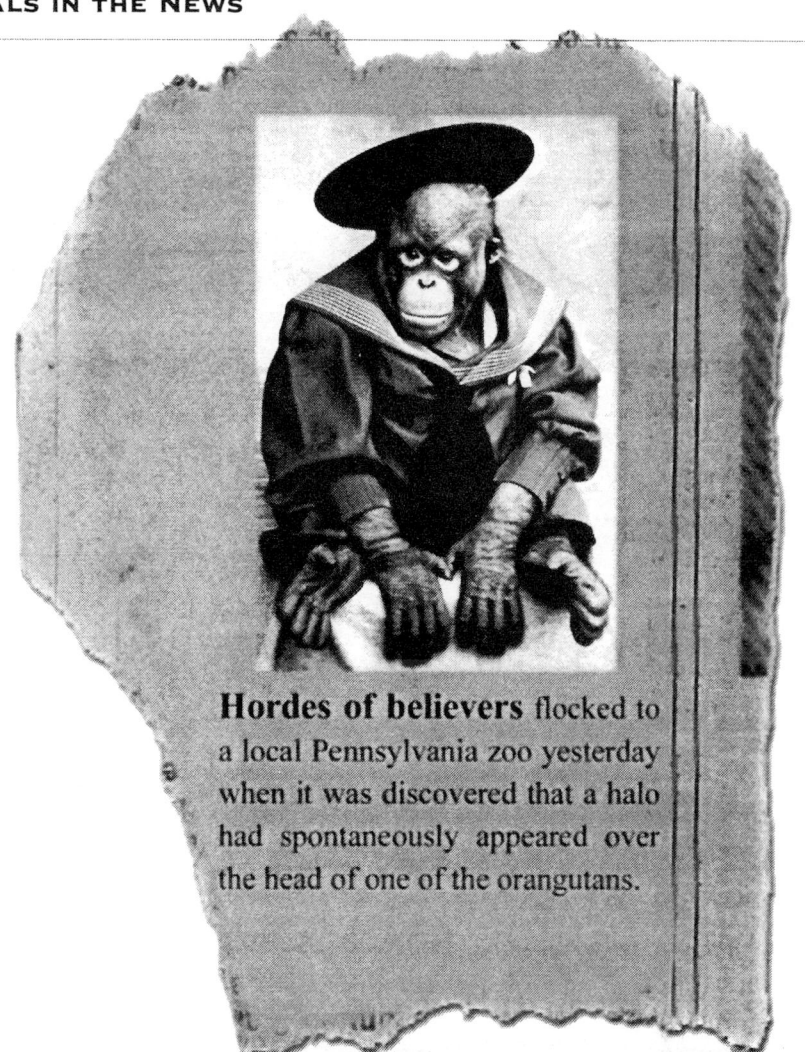

**Hordes of believers** flocked to a local Pennsylvania zoo yesterday when it was discovered that a halo had spontaneously appeared over the head of one of the orangutans.

leased yesterday show.

**The union of humor** and the media gained national attention yesterday when the chicken in this dramatic photo testified to Congress that the only reason he crossed the road was that he heard the joke on TV.

**Two beauty contestants** showed up in Oxnard, Tennessee, yesterday for the annual K-Nine beauty contest. The judges said the loser, pictured here on the left, just didn't look enough like a dog.

**In Scuttsville, Pennsylvania,** the president of the United Animals Union (right) was able to tell petting zoo employees to go to work after a six-month walkout. Workers had complained of heavy petting.

**The President's Saftly Council** released a warning this week of what can happen when you and your dog fall asleep with the backyard hose on.

**Mrs. Shelly Kipperstein** of Truckington, Florida, made the *Guinness Book of World Records* yesterday for being put on hold for four days and thirteen minutes by the Department of Moter Vehicles. Kippersttein finally got through and was told by customer service that no one likes the photo on their driver's license.

MISSING PHOTO

**According to** unnamed tabloid sources, Richard M. Nixon became so delusional during his final days in office that he truly believed, for one day, that he was an animal faith healer.

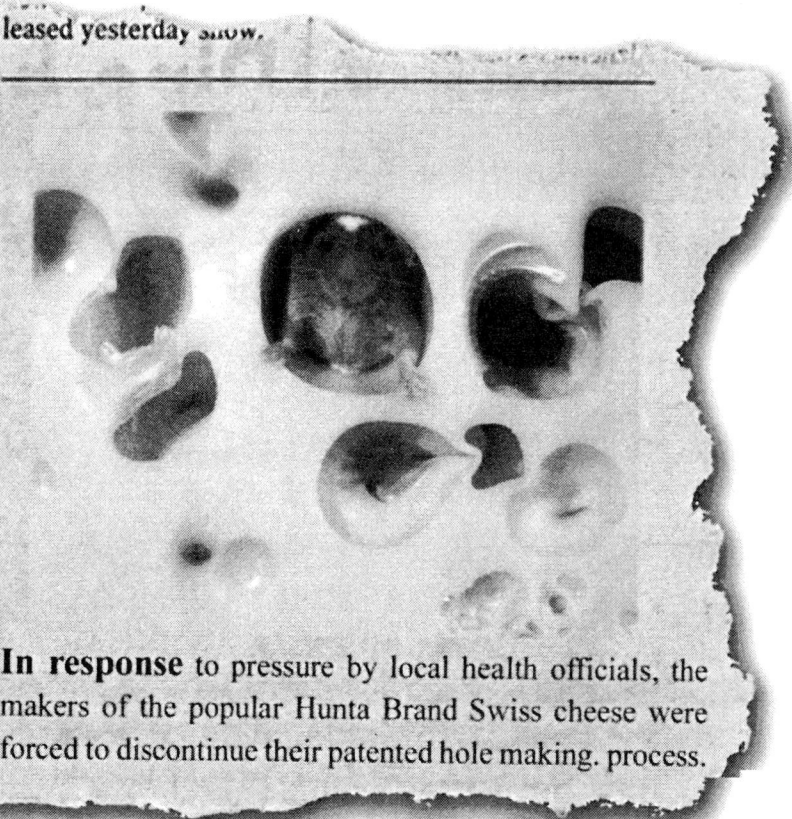

leased yesterday show.

than
much

its are
has re-
Ground-
en the
rodent

bre
ng
ch
ot
n
no

ser
nia
ct.
rd,
p,

**In response** to pressure by local health officials, the makers of the popular Hunta Brand Swiss cheese were forced to discontinue their patented hole making. process.

**At the North Pole,** explorer Sir Edmund Hammond embarrassed an entire gender of humans yesterday when he became the first man in history to ask directions.

**In Ellsmont, New Hampshire,** some neighborhood pets got together to re-create the scene from the 1981 hit movie *Chariots of Fur*.

than
much

ats are
has re-
Ground-
en the
rodent

bre
ng
eh
ot
n
no

ser
nia
ct.
rd,
p.

leased yesterday show.

**The United Bureau of Statistics** reported yesterday that because they are afraid of flying, 75 percent of all monkeys prefer to travel cross country on the greyhound.

n

d in an

Diaz,
lleg-
ed in
also
hine
d to
taten

**In Gaston, New Hampshire,** a rash of resident complaints alerted authorities to a new type of crime wave spreading across the city: peeping tom cats.

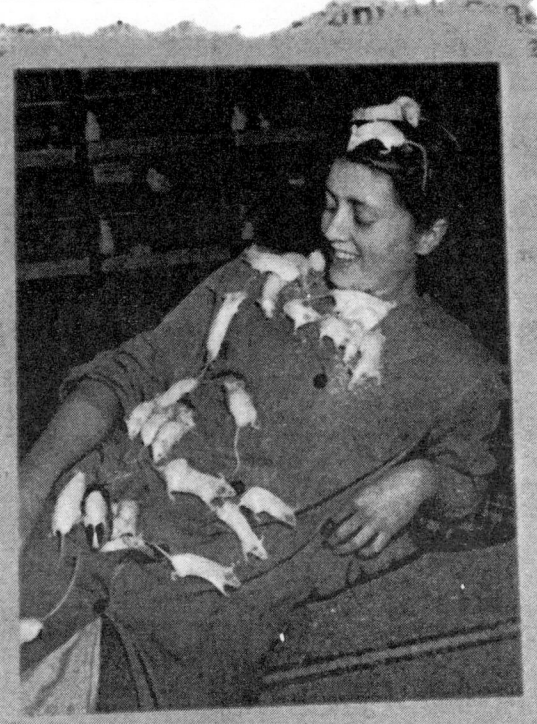

**Dairy shop employee** Marie Resnick of Blitstown, Ohio, was rushed to county medical yesterday following a strange occurrence which happened just moments after cutting the cheese.

**Eight-year-old Matthew Belich** was expelled from his Shamoikin, Tennessee, grade schhol yesterday, when it was learned that his donkey, Jeff, actually completed all of his homework assignments.

**In Kempton, Nebraska,** ten year old Diana Coterra missed the point, after being told it was wrong to put her pets in the clothes dryer.

**The owners** of a famous masonry company in Milan, Italy, were sued yesterday, when it was discovered that they were passing off live lions as stone statues for the front of rich people's mansions.

**A movie** that is stirring much controversy opened in theaters yesterday. The movie, Bark Avenue, is about a creature who's part* dog/part elderly Yiddish New York jeweler

**And a friendly reminder** from the County Board of Health. Always be sure to lather, rinse then, repeat, all of your poultry thoroughly.

**In Bombay, India,** a local clothier came under fire Tuesday, for its dangerous unconventional method of measuring men's hat sizes.

**This just in** from Roylander, Nebraska. We now have proof of something that is actually more fun than a barrel of monkeys.

**Clara and Beatrice Stone** were questioned by authorities yesterday, when it was learned that they were putting on elementary school puppet shows using real-life bears.

than
much

ts are
has re-
round-
n the
odent

re
ng
eh
t
n
no

ser
nia
ct.
rd,
p,
t

leased yesterday show.

**New Jersey resident** Les Klinman rushed his dog, Deke, to the Truesdale Veterinary Hospital yesterday, after the animal fell face-first off of his fourth-story balcony. Aside from his nose, the Greyhound showed no signs of injury.

**In Silverton, Rhode Island,** three-year-old Ashley Roberts became the youngest magician ever to perform a trick once thought impossible, pulling a live monkey from a Dixie cup.

**This just in** out in Trevor, California: Six shocked meerkats stood in disbelief as animal handler Jim Fowler chose a baby lion cub for *The Tonight Show* instead of them.

**Roscoe** the performing pooch was released from his multimillion-dollar contract yesterday, after the director complained that he kept taking the term "close-up" far too literally.

**The Shellville, Minnestota,** Police Department received an anonymous tip in the form of a photo yesterday, of missing person Ellen Hernsworth...moments before she was allegedly sucked up by an unidentified pachyderm.

her

"
aske
"
"
The
$15

thi

go
cu
be

w
qu

G
st

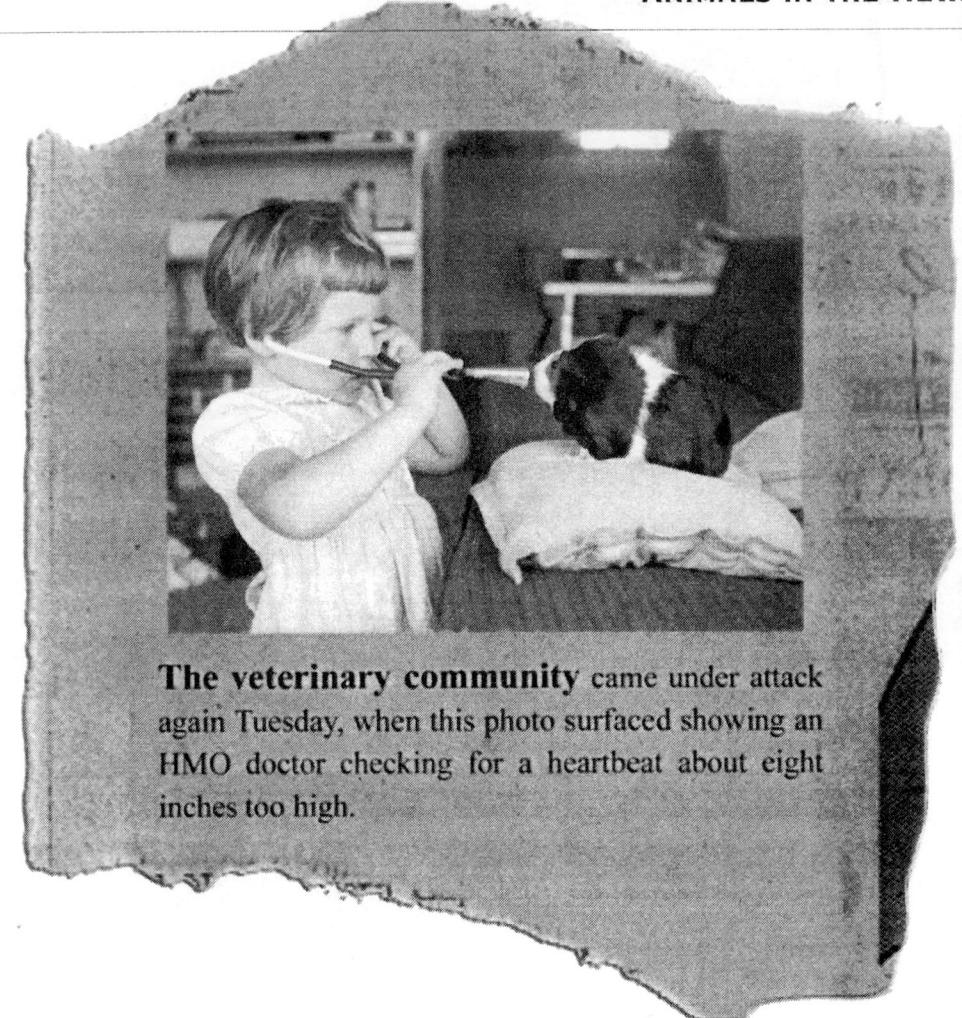

**The veterinary community** came under attack again Tuesday, when this photo surfaced showing an HMO doctor checking for a heartbeat about eight inches too high.

**Yesterday** at the Winslow County Chess Tournament, Dusty the chess playing chimp didn't know how to tell tournament officials that he accidentally swallowed one of his own pawns.

MISSING PHOTO

**In Charlot Township,** Delaware, volunteer fireman Ed Rule was fined $250 when, instead of following accepted procedure, he sent his Pit Bull, Spike, up a tree to retrieve a kitten.

**Nature photogragher** Gene Pitney never
listened to his mother and paid the hefty price.
It seems that, while making a silly face when
snapping this nature shot, it froze.

**Five-year-old Rose Karem** entered record books yesterday, when she became the youngest person to balance an egg and spoon on a Boston Terrier by merely using her mind.

**The good nature of Rusty,** the world's only literate Cocker Spaniel, quickly turned to horror when he learned that his owner had put him up for sale in the classifiede ads.